Galloway Travellers

Andrew McCormick's Tinkler-Gypsy Photographs

Loving to ramble in the open air, and fond of reading, I have already extracted sufficient reward for making this somewhat belated attempt to rescue information about the strange people treated of in the following pages. In summer my visits to camps have added zeal and excitement to many an enjoyable work in this lovely Galloway of ours. Only those who have caught the cult of Gypsyism can tell what an extraordinary charm and fascination there is in studying and reading and writing about the Gypsy race.
Andrew McCormick

This year marks the centenary of the publication of Andrew McCormick's 'The Tinkler-Gypsies of Galloway.' It was one of the first books to look at the life and culture of Scottish traveller communities and is now regarded as a classic of Galloway literature.

'The Tinkler-Gypsies' is a fascinating mixture of folk tale, popular anecdote, historical research and social observation which McCormick described as 'some gleanings along a literary Gypsy by-path.' In it he looked at the origins of the area's travellers and explored the myth and reality of Billy Marshall, the self-styled King of the Tinklers who, together with his band of travellers, was the focus of many Galloway folktales. But the main value of the book today is its presentation of traveller life in the early years of the 20th century. McCormick visited the camps, talked to individual travellers and listened to their tales. He also tried to record the 'cant' or dialect of the Galloway travellers and found many words related to Romany, the gypsy language. This convinced McCormick that Galloway's travellers shared a similar cultural background with the gypsy communities of England and Europe and led him to coin the term 'tinkler-gypsy.'

Traveller families like the Marshalls, MacMillans, Kennedies and Stewarts had been in Galloway for generations. Surviving on the margins of society, they earned a living through hawking, horse dealing, making and mending pots and pans, basket-making, horning, cockling, shellfishing and seasonal farm work. Most local travellers had a permanent winter base, often in a house, but in spring they took to the road, selling their goods and labour as they moved through Galloway, and coming together with other travellers at some of the region's long established camp sites.

Andrew McCormick (1867-1956) was a successful lawyer, a member of Newton Stewart town council and Provost of the burgh. How did someone like this, a pillar of Edwardian middle class respectability, develop such a fascination for travelling communities? Perhaps by studying and writing about travellers he was able to escape, at least in spirit, from some of the social constraints of small town Scotland. 'I have grown Gypsy-like,' he wrote in the book's Preface, 'for I have roamed about far and near to rescue and record some of the meagre information still obtainable about our tinkler-gypsies.'

A genuine interest in traveller society can be traced back to George Borrow who wrote about and occasionally lived with the English gypsies. His autobiographical works 'Lavengro' (1851) and 'Romany Rye' (1857) were hugely popular and in 1888 The Gypsy Lore Society was formed to promote the study of gypsy and traveller culture. McCormick was influenced by Borrow and the 'gypsyologists' and was obviously keen to continue their work by looking at traveller communities in his native Galloway.

One of the delights of 'The Tinkler-Gypsies of Galloway' is its extensive use of illustrations, including a large number of photographs of Galloway travellers and their camps taken by McCormick himself. Unfortunately many of the illustrations are frustratingly small – sometimes only 55 mm x 70 mm – and are often poorly reproduced and lacking in contrast.

Andrew McCormick with German gypsies at Newton Stewart in 1906.

In 1999 Andrew McCormick's daughter, Margaret, came to Stranraer Museum with a collection of over 100 glass negatives, lantern slides and prints which had just been found in the back of a safe at the firm of McCormick and Nicholson in Newton Stewart. These were some of the original images used in 'The Tinkler-Gypsies' together with a number of unpublished photographs of Galloway travellers and English and European gypsies. Miss McCormick readily gave her permission for the collection to be copied by the Dumfries and Galloway Museums Service and a selection is reproduced in this booklet. Quotes from 'The Tinkler-Gypsies of Galloway' are shown in italics.

John Pickin, Stranraer Museum. 2006.

The sketch (left) for the title page of 'The Tinkler-Gypsies of Galloway' shows a traveller family at Blackcraig, Newton Stewart. The illustrator, Dr Hamilton Irving of Huddersfield, must have used Andrew McCormick's photograph (above right) as inspiration because the horse, traces and wagon are a direct copy. Unfortunately we have no information on the family shown in the photograph.

The sketch includes the figure of a priest following the wagon. This might refer to the Catholic priest who appears in *Lavengro*, the autobiography of the Victorian writer and gypsyologist George Borrow. McCormick was influenced by Borrow's work and published an article in *The Gallovidian* magazine on his mentor's tour through Galloway in 1866.

Most of the travellers that McCormick met and interviewed came from Galloway. He built up particularly good relations with the Marshalls and here we see William Marshall, patriarch of the family, and his wife Katie O'Neil.

There can be no doubt that the Marshalls have also Gypsy blood in their veins. The appearance of the various members of the family prove it, and the presence of many Romani words in their cant confirms it. Tradition related that the Marshalls have been tinklers in Galloway since time out of mind; and it is likely there were tinkler Marshalls in Galloway in 1505.

Two more views (left and above) of the Marshall family. They were McCormick's main source of information on traveller cant and dialect.

Often as the reader may have seen and conversed with the Marshalls, MacMillans and other tinkler-gypsies who frequent Galloway, did he ever imagine that they posses the remnants of a language unknown to ordinary Gallovidians? It was only last summer (1905), so the Marshalls say, that any outsiders have learned from them that they possess a speech or 'cant' of their own in which there are many Romani words.

William Marshall and some of his extended family on the road between Newton Stewart and Creetown. Blackcraig Hill is in the distance.

The wagon is typical of the sort used by Galloway travellers and held all the family's possessions – bedding, clothing, pots, pans, plates and cooking gear. When fully loaded there would have been little room for passengers and most members of a travelling family had little choice but to walk alongside. The wagon has a canvas cover over timber hoops; this could be lifted from the vehicle and, as shown in other photographs in this booklet, used as tent.

McCormick's original caption for this was '"King William" foots it gaily.'

A Cumberland tinkler and a Carlisle lad who were travelling in company as clog dancers next favoured the company with a breakdown. One of the two played a mouthharmonium as they danced. This merely served to whet the appetite of William, the King of the Marshall gang, and he speedily formed a square for a reel. He and his consort were partners and soon amidst much hooching and yells of laughter, they were cleeking and swinging and footing gaily the jolliest reel imaginable.

This bonneted figure clipping a sheet of horn with a pair of shears is Francie Marshall from Kirkcowan. Horn working, especially carving and turning horn spoons, was a traditional tinkler craft.

Cow horns were mostly used; rams' horns are more difficult to work, though more durable. Like the tailors of old who went out to "whip the cat" for months at a time, the Marshalls travelled from farm-house to farm-house working up the rams' horns for farmers for board and so much money.

McCormick called this image 'Marshalls: hardy upbringing.' It was probably taken at Silver Hill, Blackcraig. The covered top has been removed from the wagon to provide shelter. Blankets and oil-cloth are spread over a layer of rushes but there is nothing else to protect the family from the damp ground. There are few personal possessions. This, of all McCormick's photographs, comes closest to capturing the harsh reality of life for Galloway's travellers.

Geordie said, "We'll soon be driven off the road."
"Deed aye, faith," echoed his wife.
"Na," objected Leezie Marshall, who was nursing a baby, "They're no fit to do that, but they micht make us, in the interest o' oor bairns, hae oor beds twa feet aff the grun'."
"Deed aye," agreed Mrs MacMillan, "There's many a yin meets his death wi' sleepin' on wat strae."

The MacMillans were another of the local traveller families. This is Mary MacMillan and her un-named partner, a veteran of the Crimean war.

Old Grannie is a treat to listen to, and is possessed with the most useful gift a tinkler can possess – that of eloquence. Daily she shoulders her rooskie (hawker's basket) and goes from door to door extolling her small wares, for, frail though she be, she is credited with not having a lazy bone in her body.

She was 75 when these photographs were taken and had been forced by ill health to move into a common lodging-house.

During the summer months many of the traveller families met up at a series of traditional camp sites. Parliament Knowe above Kirroughtree was the favoured site at Newton Stewart. There were others at Glenluce, Creetown and The Doon, Kirkcudbright. Hightae, close to Dumfries, was another traditional meeting place.

This view shows members of the Watson, MacMillan and Marshall families.

Another view of one of the Newton Stewart camps. Leezie MacMillan, who appears in a number of the photographs, is the woman on the right with the baby.

Soon the members of the other gangs all began to drop in from the labours of the day, the women folk from selling tin ware made by the men, or from selling small drapery goods which they carried in rooskies (baskets), and the men from selling wax cloth or brushes, or from horse-dealing, or as is too often the case, from having a carousal.

Many of the illustrations in 'The Tinkler-Gypsies of Galloway' appear to have been dropped in at random and have little or no association with the text. These three well-dressed girls who we see dancing a jig and standing with a proud adult are an example. They are Watsons, perhaps part of an English travelling family, but we know nothing else about them.

A remarkable image of four traveller families together at Newton Stewart. Here are Perthshire Stewarts, Argyllshire Cambells, Cumberland Morrisons and Galloway Marshalls.

There is a certain breezy light-heartedness about the tinkler that enables him to rise superior to the misery of his lot. Their upbringing is of the hardiest order: miserable shelter from exposure; always on the border of starvation, and yet they are not usually prone to commit other than the most trifling offences.

William Marshall, left, with two other Scottish travellers. The woman is a Stewart from Perthshire and the man a Cambell from Argyll. Like Galloway, Argyll and Perthshire at the turn of the 20th century were home to a large number of traveller families. Stewarts still form part of the traveller scene in north-east Scotland today.

The Wilson family.
Like most traveller communities, Galloway travellers were quite superstitious.

They deem it very lucky to be first-footed by a donkey or a sheep, but particularly the former; indeed, one of the gang generally makes it his duty to lead the cuddy into the house first thing on New Year's morning. One tinkler woman told the writer that all the Marshalls she ever knew believed in witches. When asked why she kept two little shoes – a cuddy's and a donkey's - hanging behind the door, she at once replied, "To keep out the witches."

The Stewart family at Newton Stewart. The cast iron kettle and cooking pot are on the camp fire, wicker hampers and a high-backed chair have been taken from the wagon, and a half-finished meal sits on a fold of oilcloth spread out on the ground.

McCormick called this view 'Breakfast Time.'

Isabella, one of the Galloway Stewarts, posing outside the family's living wagon with a dog of very doubtful pedigree.

McCormick's title was 'On Guard.'

McCormick met this woman, a Stewart from the Highlands, at Parliament Knowe.

A poor old shrivelled mite of a woman was squatting on the ground in the mouth of the tent. Her frock was in tatters and hung loosely on her shrunken frame. Her garment bodice being open at the neck showed that she wore little or no underclothing. A cutty pipe was in her mouth, and if clouds of smoke mean aught she was enjoying her smoke.

"Barrie davies, gran-maismort"
(Fine day, grannie), I said.
"Tis that kind sir," she said, turning her sightless face towards me.
"Don't you know cant, grannie?"
"Oh aye dear, bit I seldom speak it."
"Why?" I asked.
"Oh, it's juist no nice."

Two views of the Parliament Knowe camp at Newton Stewart.

"And how're you, Geordie?"
"I'm weel," said he, "an' I was juist telling my mither before I left Parliament Knowe that it was in this shan wee gav (bad wee town) that the young man who was interested in travellers leeved. Dae ye ken what she said, young man?"
"No," said I.
"Weel, she said that he maun be a rauge gadgi (daft man) that wad ha'e ocht to do wi' tinklers".

This couple are standing with their stock in trade - rolls of linoleum floor covering. Lino, made by coating a backing of woven jute with a mixture of powdered cork, linseed oil, roisin and pigment, was produced mainly in Kirkcaldy. The couple probably travelled to Fife to buy lino direct from the factories.

This photograph appears in the book with the caption 'Pretty Partners' but there is nothing in the text to identify these two well-dressed traveller girls.

The girls seen in the previous image appear again in this photograph. They are posing with woven mats and what appears to be a roll of printed wallpaper. The girls probably travelled from farm to farm and around the villages selling floor coverings.

Travellers like Mary MacMillan were great story tellers.

A born folk-tale teller, but one wants to hear and see her tell her tales fully to appreciate them. The grip she takes of her words, her intonation, attitudes and gestures, all make for a fuller comprehension and enjoyment of the tale. Some of these she spins out for hours and never halts for a word.

English travellers were common visitors to Galloway. Here an English family sits around the camp fire as the father carves clothes pegs. The top has been taken from the wagon – it will be used to shelter two adults and four young children.

This photograph was taken by James Dunn, a Newton Stewart chemist, and used by McCormick in 'The Tinkler Gypsies.' McConchie of Kirkcudbright was another local photographer who took images of travellers. He sold a number of popular views showing the camp at The Doon, Nun Mill, Kirkcudbright.

A group of English gypsies with a typically ornate wagon or varda.

About 30 years ago a large band of English gypsies visited Galloway. Horse-dealing was the occupation of the men, and the women told fortunes. There was a large company on that occasion, and they encamped for several weeks in a field – which they had rented – near Newton Stewart. Crowds of people flocked to visit their encampment, and people still speak of some of that company being the handsomest men and women they have ever seen.

The arrival of 'real' English gypsies was an opportunity for McCormick to test his knowledge of the Romany language.

I naturally enquired whether Mrs C (shown here with the milk can) spoke the Romani language.
"Is it really a language?" I enquired.
"Oh, yes; it is not jargon like what tinklers, potters, and showmen speak. We have names for almost everything, but we don't like outsiders to get to know our language."

Mrs 'C' the English gypsy and her daughters.

I thought it would be interesting to contrast the appearance of Romanies with those of tinkler-gypsies, and I again – this time with camera in hand – visited the Chuministos' living wagon.
Raising my hat, I enquired at Mrs C if they were in the habit of distributing photos of themselves. "No sir," she replied, "and we resent any attempts to snapshot us."
I then thought I must take other means if I wished to secure a photo, and it occurred to me that the best thing I could do was to tell her I wished, by photographs, as illustrations, to show the unmistakable difference between tinkler-gypsies and Romanies. The idea was a happy one, and appealed to her.

In July 1906 a group of Calderari gypsies from Germany passed through Galloway. McCormick visited them with a German-speaking interpreter.

The prospect of a visit to a gypsy encampment always thrills me with a delightful excitement, and the fact of my Gypsies being on this occasion foreigners, and the Romanes differing widely from English Romanes, made my proposed visit unusually exciting.

The Queen – Marono-Dammo – did us the honour of dressing specially to have her photo taken, and donned a lovely shawl, asking my lady friend if it was not 'sehr schones Tuch' (a very pretty shawl) and indicating to me in Romanes the various colours – kaulo (black), selno (green), lollo (red), and so forth. One of the Romani-chals (boys) caused considerable amusement by shouting in most approved Galloway dialect to a boy who was likely to spoil the photo "Haud oot o' the road, boych."

McCormick was fascinated by the German gypsies but not everyone in Newton Stewart shared his enthusiasm.

Of course their visit produced the usual furore. Doors were bolted, and cannie shopkeepers either blocked the entrance to their shops with their own manly forms, or, deeming discretion the better part of valor, put the key of the door in their pockets, and stood on the footpath feigning that they had no connection with the shop.

A group of East European gypsies at Hazlewood, Creetown. These are Ursari or bear-leader gypsies and the head of one of their performing bears can just be made out below the tree on the left. They toured Galloway in 1896.

'Near Kirkcudbright I met a large troup of gypsies, of a type quite different from any I had met before. The first to appear round a corner was a tall, swarthy man leading a brown bear. My dog, a big, powerful beast, immediately made a rush for the bear but I managed to catch him in time. The man came up and, in very broken English, said the bear would not hurt the dog. I explained that my fears were not for the dog but for the bear, an under-sized, emaciated beast, and strongly muzzled.'
McCormick took this quote from F H Groome's 'Gypsy Folk Tales'. The photograph was taken by A McNeur.

Another image of Ursari gypsies with their bears. Unfortunately we don't know where this photograph was taken and it may not be a McCormick original. The Ursari group described in 'The Tinkler-Gypsies' came from Romania and travelled across northern England and southern Scotland between 1895 and 1897.

'They were very dark in colour, like Hindoos: the men and the older women were aquiline in features; some of the younger girls really beautiful, with lithe, graceful figures; all had splendid teeth.'

"Have you no other word for a cuddy?" I asked (William Marshall).
"Aye, a genetan (half-breed mule)," he curtly replied.
"Just one moment," I intervened, "would you call it an aizel or an oozel?" Smiling frankly he came back to my desk and said "We ca't an oozel, but losh bless me, whaur have ye picked that up?"
His fit of uneasiness had passed and for upwards of two hours he communicated to me the cant words of the tinkler-gypsies of Galloway".

This old couple travelled the countryside collecting bottles which they exchanged for paper flags. The man came from Marseilles, was a tailor by trade and had fought in the American Civil War.

I had gone up to the old man and said – "What's an aizel (tinklers' cant for donkey) and he at once pointed to his donkey and said – "That's one." Then I said – "You are tinklers then?" "No," he rejoined, "we are bad and bad enough; but, thank God, we are not so low down as tinklers." "Well," I said, "aizel is tinklers' cant." "That may be, but it's German tongue, and if you want German, French or Holland tongue, come to me and I can give it to you grammatical true."

More Marshalls. The boy shown in the photograph to the left is another Marshall but we know nothing else about him. The group around the campfire (above) are also Marshalls and the man sitting on the left with a child is probably Geordie Marshall.

Young Geordie MacMillan may be taken as a good specimen of the MacMillan gang. He is a strong, active fellow, who has travelled both in the Highlands and Lowlands of Scotland, and part of England and Wales, and has spent some considerable time in Canada. He was married to a cousin of his own in Pictou, Canada. His ruddy complexion, black hair, dark eyes, quick inquisitive glance, and his restless manner all go to show that there is, for a tinkler, an unusually large proportion of gypsy blood in his veins.

Andrew McCormick and Mary MacMillan